INSTANT BASS

DANNY MORRIS

Edited by
JONATHAN FEIST

Berklee Press

Director: Dave Kusek
Managing Editor: Debbie Cavalier
Marketing Manager: Ola Frank
Sr. Writer/Editor: Jonathan Feist
Writer/Editor: Susan Gedutis
Project Manager: Ilene Altman

ISBN 0-634-01667-9

1140 Boylston Street
Boston, MA 02215-3693 USA
(617) 747-2146

Visit Berklee Press Online at
www.berkleepress.com

DISTRIBUTED BY

HAL•LEONARD®
CORPORATION
7777 W. BLUEMOUND RD. P.O. BOX 13819
MILWAUKEE, WISCONSIN 53213

Visit Hal Leonard Online at
www.halleonard.com

INSTANT BASS

DANNY MORRIS

Edited by
Jonathan Feist

Contents

Dedication

To my son Charles

CD Tracks

The Band

Dan Bowden, *Guitars*   Danny Morris, *Bass*
Larry Finn, *Drums*   Malcolm Walsh, *Keyboards*

Basics

CD 01. Tuning Notes G
CD 02. Tuning Notes D
CD 03. Tuning Notes A
CD 04. Tuning Notes E

Lesson 1. Playing a Note

CD 05. Open E (then muted)
CD 06. "E Rock" Full Band
CD 07. "E Rock" Play Along

Lesson 2. Keeping Time

CD 08. E Whole Note with Bass Drum
CD 09. "Whole E Rock" Full Band
CD 10. "Whole E Rock" Play Along
CD 11. "Rock A-Round" Full Band
CD 12. "Rock A-Round" Play Along
CD 13. "Anthem" Full Band
CD 14. "Anthem" Play Along

Lesson 3. Fretted Notes

CD 15. "First Half" Full Band
CD 16. "First Half" Play Along
CD 17. "Second Half" Full Band
CD 18. "Second Half" Play Along
CD 19. "Final Score" Full Band
CD 20. "Final Score" Play Along

Lesson 4. Connecting the Dots

CD 21. "Dot Com" Full Band
CD 22. "Dot Com" Play Along

Lesson 5. Riffs

CD 23. "Duck's Riff" Full Band
CD 24. "Duck's Riff" Play Along
CD 25. "Al's Riff" Full Band
CD 26. "Al's Riff" Play Along
CD 27. "Stax Riff" Full Band
CD 28. "Stax Riff" Play Along

Lesson 6. Fifths

CD 29. "Lo Five" Full Band
CD 30. "Lo Five" Play Along

CD 31. "High Five" Full Band
CD 32. "High Five" Play Along
CD 33. "Country Vibe" Full Band
CD 34. "Country Vibe" Play Along
CD 35. "Palm Tree" Full Band
CD 36. "Palm Tree" Play Along

Lesson 7. Eighth-Note Rhythms

CD 37. "I-M Me" Full Band
CD 38. "I-M Me" Play Along
CD 39. "Alternative Fingers" Full Band
CD 40. "Alternative Fingers" Play Along

Lesson 8. Rests

CD 41. "Whole-D Funk" Full Band
CD 42. "Whole-D Funk" Play Along
CD 43. "To The Bridge" Full Band
CD 44. "To The Bridge" Play Along

Lesson 9. Smaller Steps

CD 45. "Backwards Rap" Full Band
CD 46. "Backwards Rap" Play Along
CD 47. "Rhythm 'n' Spice" Full Band
CD 48. "Rhythm 'n' Spice" Play Along

Lesson 10. Octaves

CD 49. Octave A
CD 50. "Too Tall's Stride" Full Band
CD 51. "Too Tall's Stride" Play Along
CD 52. Octave Slide
CD 53. "Too Tall's Slide" Full Band
CD 54. "Too Tall's Slide" Play Along
CD 55. "Too Tall's Tale" Full Band
CD 56. "Too Tall's Tale" Play Along
CD 57. "Dot's Octaves" Full Band
CD 58. "Dot's Octaves" Play Along
CD 59. "Octopus" Full Band
CD 60. "Octopus" Play Along
CD 61. "Jimi's Tune" Full Band
CD 62. "Jimi's Tune" Play Along
CD 63. "Encore Octaves" Full Band
CD 64. "Encore Octaves" Play Along

Welcome to Instant Bass

This book will get you playing the bass instantly. Some friends and I put together a band, and we recorded some really fun music. The *Instant Bass CD* has songs ready for you to play along with right now!

For each tune, first check out CD tracks marked "Listen," which have me playing bass. Then, once you've learned the bass parts, it's your turn. Tracks marked "Play" have no bass part.

So get your bass out of its case and let's play some music!

Basics

The Bass

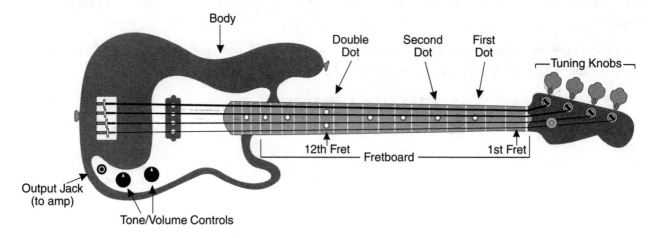

Other equipment needed: bass amplifier, 1/4" cable, CD player.

Plugging In

1. With the amplifier off, set all knobs to the twelve o'clock position. Set the master volume to zero.

2. Plug the cable into your bass. Plug the other end into the amp's input.

3. Turn on the amp.

4. Turn the bass's volume knob up all the way and pluck a string. You should not hear anything.

5. Slowly turn up the amp's master volume. Pluck a string. Find an amp volume setting that lets you hear the bass comfortably.

6. You can always lower the volume on your bass once the amp is set up.

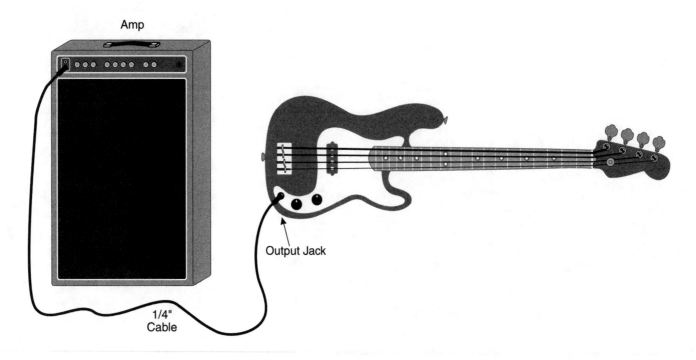

Strings

The bass has four strings—from lowest sounding to highest sounding: E, A, D, G. The strings are shown as they appear when you look down at the bass, while you are in playing position.

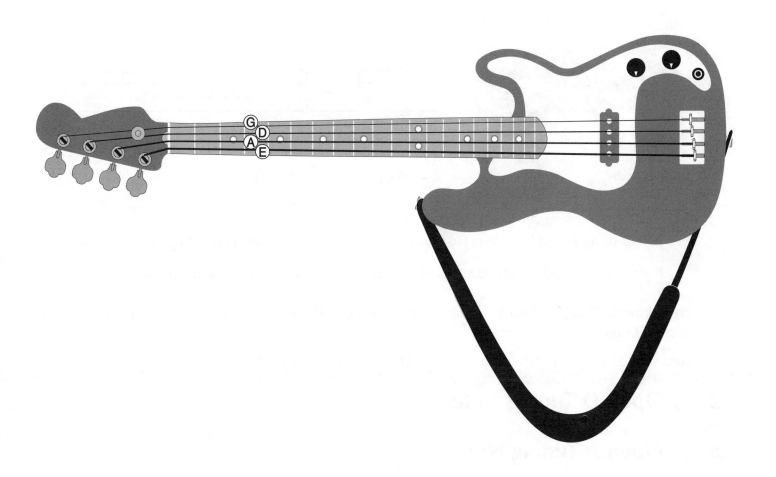

Tuning

There are lots of ways to tune. Here's how to do it with the CD.

1 1. Open G Tuning Note

1. Listen to CD track 1. Play the open G string on your bass.

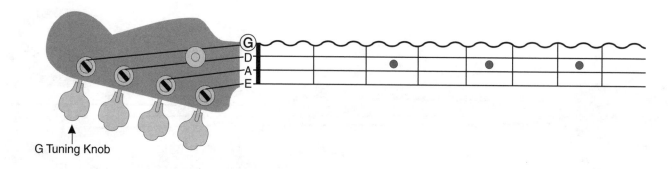

2. To make these two G notes the same, determine whether the pitch of your G string is above or below the tuned pitch on the CD.

3. While the G string sounds, turn its tuning knob until the string is at the same pitch as the CD's tuning note.

G Tuning Knob

If your string sounds lower than the CD (flat), it is too loose, so tighten the tuning knob.

If your string sounds higher than the CD (sharp), it is too tight, so loosen the tuning knob.

Try to hear the "beats" as your bass note gets closer to being in tune. When your string is tuned, the beats will stop.

Tune your other three strings in the same way, and you're ready to play!

2 2. Open D Tuning Note

3 3. Open A Tuning Note

4 4. Open E Tuning Note

Lesson One **Playing a Note**

Open E

The open E is the lowest and biggest string.

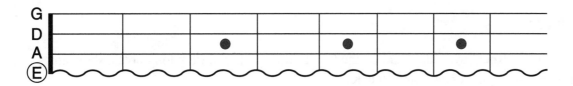

5 Listen to the sound of an open E, and then play it yourself. Pluck it with your right-hand index finger.

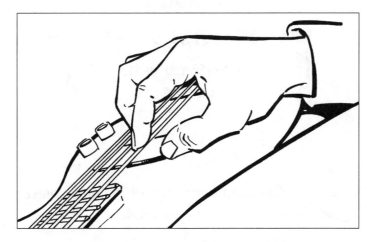

> ***Tip:*** *Scratch your head. Move your finger the same way when you play a string.*

Muting

To mute (silence) a string, touch it with your left hand.

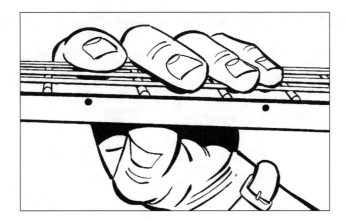

Play!

Play an open E and then mute it. You may hear a ringing in the other strings when playing open E. Touch them to mute this ringing.

E Rock

This first tune, "E Rock," is played on the open-string E.

6 1. Listen

If you can play an open E, you can play this tune. Listen to the bass on the CD. All it plays is the open E string.

7 2. Play

Now, play "E Rock" with the band on the CD. Follow your ear. Play long notes, short notes, loud or soft notes—just play open E and ROCK!

E ROCK

ROCK

‖: PLAY OPEN E
WHENEVER YOU WANT.
FOLLOW YOUR EAR. :‖

 Your most important job as a bass player is to play the bottom notes.

Lesson Two **Keeping Time**

Whole Notes

This is an E *whole note* (𝅝). It lasts four beats. Count "1 2 3 4."

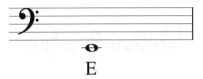

E

8 1. Listen

Listen to the bass drum. It plays four beats while the bass holds each E whole note. The bass plays with the drums on beat 1 of every bar. Count along as you listen.

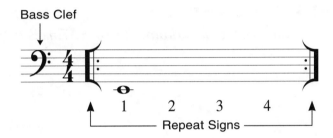

Tip: *When you see these signs* ⦗: :⦘ *, repeat the music between them.*

3

Whole E Rock

9 **1. Listen**

This tune is like "E Rock," but the bass plays steady whole notes.

10 **2. Play**

Play along with "Whole E Rock." Hook up with the bass drum on beat 1 of every bar.

> **Tip:** Play at **exactly** the same time as the bass drum on beat 1. This is called "hooking up."

Open A

Play an open-string A.

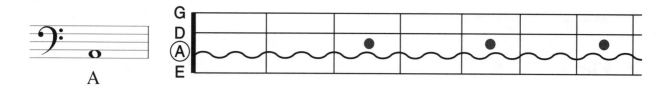

A

Rock A-Round

11 1. Listen

This bass part is like the one in "Whole E Rock," but it is played on the open A string.

12 2. Play

Hook up with the bass drum on beat 1. Let your open A ring for beats 2, 3, and 4.

ROCK A-ROUND

Anthem

13 1. Listen

This bass part combines open E and open A.

14 2. Play

Make sure you mute your strings before playing the next note.

ANTHEM

𝄢 *A bassist has to keep steady time.*

Fretted Notes

First Dot: G

To change a string's note, press the string all the way down on the fretboard between any two fret bars.

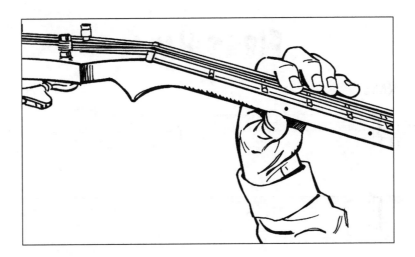

Play the note "G" on the E string at the first dot (third fret). Hold down the string with your left index finger.

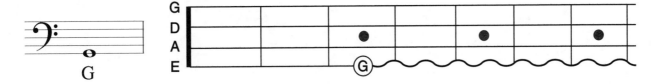

Tablature

Tablature (or just "tab") shows a note's fret. Tab has four lines, showing the four strings. On the lines are numbers, showing what fret you should press to get the note.

Here is G with its tablature. It looks like the fretboard diagrams you have been reading.

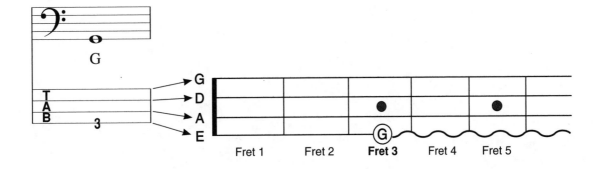

First Half

15 **1. Listen**

Count along while you listen, "1 2 3 4, 1 2 3 4, ..."

16 **2. Play**

Play an open E whole note. Then play a G whole note. That's all you need to play this tune.

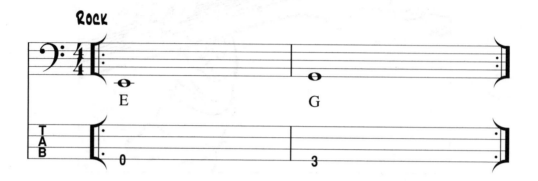

First Dot: C

Play the note "C" on the A string at the first dot (third fret). Hold down the string with your left index finger.

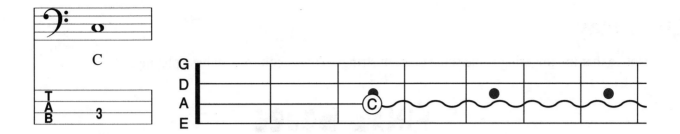

Second Half

17 1. Listen

Count along while you listen, "1 2 3 4."

18 2. Play

Play an open A whole note. Then play a C whole note. That's all you need to play "Second Half."

SECOND HALF

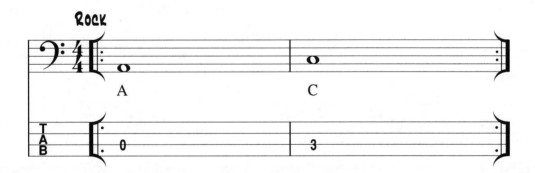

Final Score

19 **1. Listen**

"Final Score" combines the bass lines from "First Half" and "Second Half."

20 **2. Play**

Notice that the fingering is the same on both strings. This is common in bass playing.

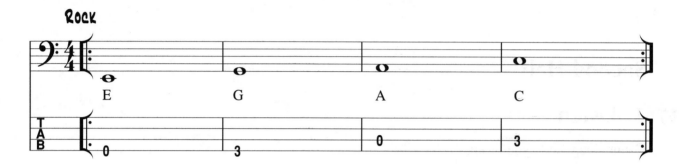

Bass and drums play the music's foundation.

Connecting the Dots

Second Dot: A and D

Find A on the E string, second dot (fifth fret).

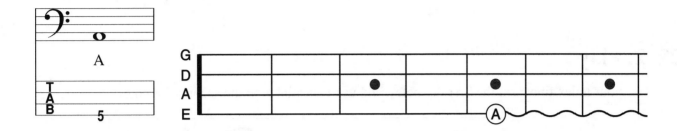

Find D on the A string, second dot (fifth fret).

The next tune, "Dot Com," combines notes on the first and second dots.

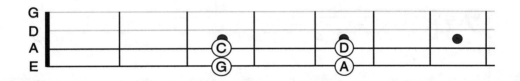

Dot Com

21 1. Listen

Follow the music as you listen to this tune. The bass plays *half notes*. Half notes (♩) get two beats.

> **Tip:** Count along with the beat, "1 2 3 4." This will help you hook up with the rest of the band, and get you inside the song's rhythm.

22 2. Play

Use your index finger on the first-dot notes, and use your pinky on the second-dot notes.

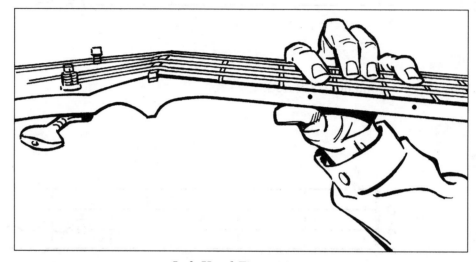

Left-Hand Fingering

DOT COM

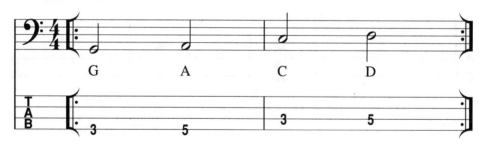

> **Tip:** Notice that these notes form a "box" pattern on the fretboard. Remembering patterns is easier than remembering notes.

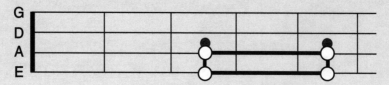

Riffs are repeated patterns of notes. This next bass line is a riff that uses three notes on the E string: open E, G first dot (third fret), and A second dot (fifth fret).

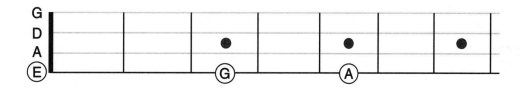

Duck's Riff

23 1. Listen

Follow the music as you listen to this tune. The bass plays *quarter notes.* Quarter notes (♩) get one beat.

24 2. Play

DUCK'S RIFF

RHYTHM 'N' BLUES

Moving the Pattern

This riff is the same pattern used in "Duck's Riff," but it is on the A string.

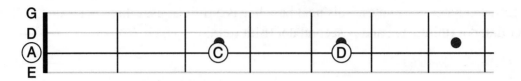

Al's Riff

25 ### 1. Listen

Listen to the steady quarter notes.

26 ### 2. Play

Stax Riff

27 ### 1. Listen

This tune uses the same riff.

28 ### 2. Play

First, play "Duck's Riff." Then play "Al's Riff." Keep this eight-bar pattern repeating and WALK THAT BASS!

STAX RIFF

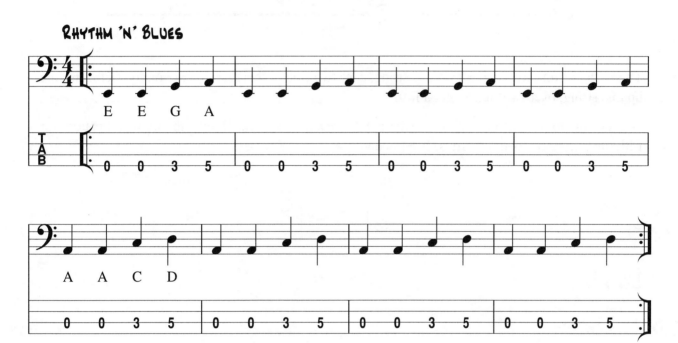

On the Scene

Bassist Duck Dunn and drummer Al Jackson played on many hit recordings for the Stax label. Bass/drum grooves like this one serve as the foundation for many songs.

Fifths are used in lots of bass lines. Once you know the pattern, you can play them anywhere on the fretboard.

1. Play G on the E string, first dot (third fret).

2. Play its fifth, D on the A string, second dot (fifth fret).

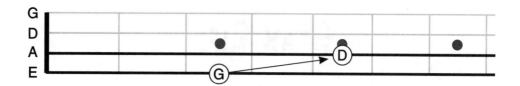

This is how fifths are fingered: up one string, over two frets. Wherever you are on the fretboard, play up one string, over two frets to get a fifth.

A good way to play a fifth is by remembering its *fretboard pattern*. Here is the fretboard pattern for a fifth: up one string, over two frets. It starts on the E string, first dot.

Lo Five

29 **1. Listen**

30 **2. Play**

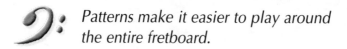
Patterns make it easier to play around the entire fretboard.

Moving the Pattern

This next tune also uses fifths, just moved to different strings. Remember the fretboard pattern for fifths:

This is the same pattern as "Lo Five."

1. Play C on the A string, first dot (third fret).

2. Play its fifth, G on the D string, second dot (fifth fret).

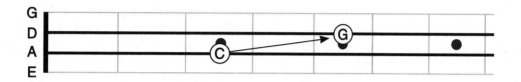

High Five

31 **1. Listen**

32 **2. Play**

HIGH FIVE

Moving the Pattern

This tune uses the same fifth patterns from "Lo Five" and "High Five."

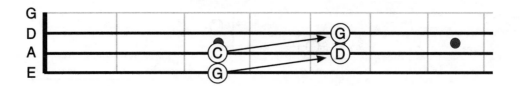

Country Vibe

33 **1. Listen**

34 **2. Play**

COUNTRY VIBE

COUNTRY ROCK

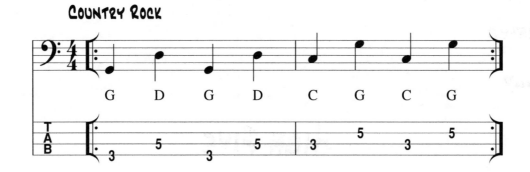

Moving the Pattern

"Palm Tree" has a Caribbean beat. Bass lines built on fifths are common in Caribbean music.

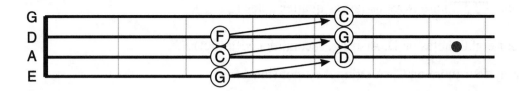

Palm Tree

35 1. Listen

36 2. Play

PALM TREE

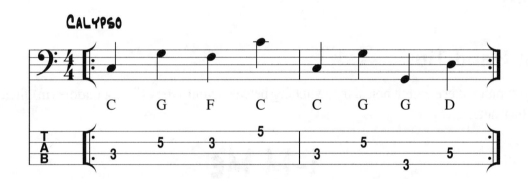

Eighth-Note Rhythms

Eighth notes (♪♪♪♪) are twice as fast as quarter notes (♩   ♩).

1. Play four eighth notes on D, A string, second dot (fifth fret).

2. Then play four more on C, A string, first dot (third fret).

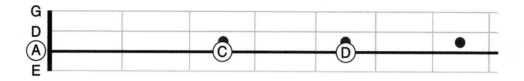

I-M Me

35 **1. Listen**

36 **2. Play**

Right-Hand Tip

When you pluck these eighth notes, try switching between your index (i) and middle (m) fingers, every other note.

I-M Me

𝄢 *Listen to the drums and play steady eighth notes.*

Growing the Riff

This tune also uses eighth-note rhythms. The bass line has one more note: F (first dot, D string).

1. The first bar is the same as "I-M Me."

2. In the second bar, play four Fs on the D string, first dot (third fret). Then play four Ds (A string, second dot).

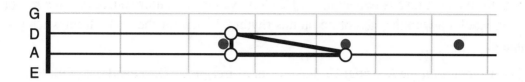

Alternative Fingers

39 **1. Listen**

40 **2. Play**

ALTERNATIVE FINGERS

ALTERNATIVE ROCK

Keep steady time. It will help your whole band to hook up.

Quarter Rest

Rests mean "don't play." When you see a rest, mute your strings.

The rhythm for the next tune is two eighths (♫) followed by a quarter rest. A *quarter rest* (𝄽) lasts for one beat. Hook up with the bass drum on this rhythm. Listen for the snare drum when you rest on beats 2 and 4.

You'll play two notes on the A string: C, first dot (third fret), then D, second dot (fifth fret).

Whole-D Funk

41 **1. Listen**

42 **2. Play**

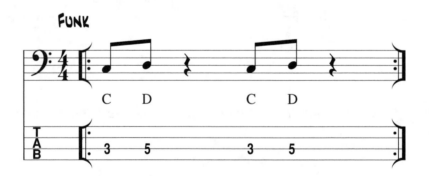

𝄢 *Lock in with the funky drummer.*

Growing the Riff

This tune also uses eighth notes and rests.

1. The first pattern is the same as "Whole-D Funk."

2. When the band yells, "TAKE IT TO THE BRIDGE!" play the same pattern on the D string. The first note is F, first dot (third fret). The second note is G, second dot (fifth fret).

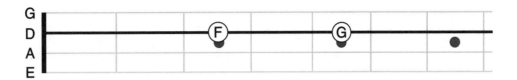

To the Bridge

43 **1. Listen**

44 **2. Play**

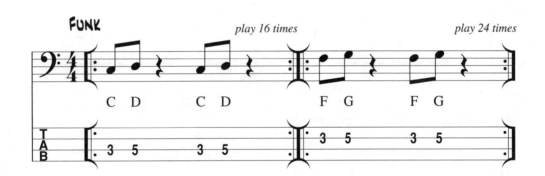

> ### *On the Scene*
>
> *James Brown, the Godfather of Soul, liked to shout, "Take it to the bridge!"*

Smaller Steps

Fretboard Pattern: Half Step

To play a half step anywhere on the fretboard, go to the next fret on the same string.

This tune moves in half steps.

Start on A, E string, second dot (fifth fret).

Move down a half step. Play A♭, back one fret.

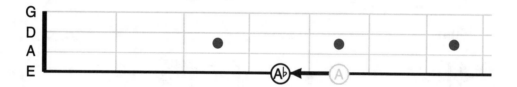

Move down a half step. Play G, back one fret.

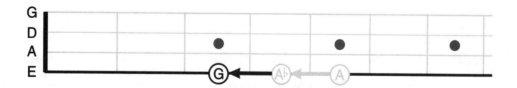

Move down a half step. Play G♭, back one fret.

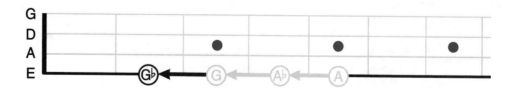

Backwards Rap

45 **1. Listen**

46 **2. Play**

BACKWARDS RAP

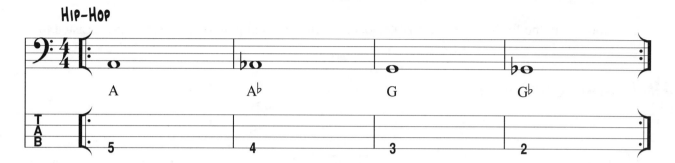

Practice your dance steps while playing these half steps.

Growing the Riff

This tune has the same notes, but this rhythm:

The bass hooks up with the bass drum. When the bass rests, the snare drum plays (beats 2 and 4). Mute your strings during rests.

Rhythm 'n' Spice

47 **1. Listen**

48 **2. Play**

RHYTHM 'N' SPICE

Playing Octaves

Octaves are the same notes, just higher or lower. To play octaves from the open strings, use the double dots (twelfth fret).

1. Play open A.

2. Now go up the fretboard to the double dots (twelfth fret) and play the A up an octave. Listen to low A and its octave.

49 Listen: Octave A

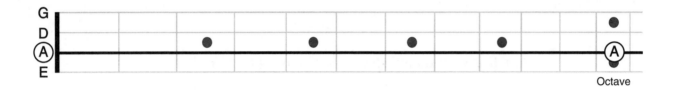

Octave

Too Tall's Stride

The bass line to "Too Tall's Stride" uses octave leaps. Play along with the recording.

50 1. Listen

51 2. Play

TOO TALL'S STRIDE

Slide

Sliding up and down the fretboard is fun and sounds great. To slide, play a high note, such as the A at the double dots, and then slide down the neck. Listen to the octave slide from high A.

52 Listen: Octave Slide

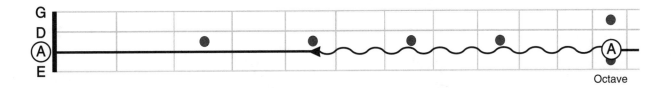

In notation, a slide looks like this:

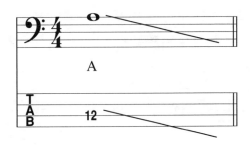

This next tune uses octaves and slides.

1. Play open A, then its octave at the double dots (twelfth fret). Then SLIDE!

2. Play open D, then its octave at the double dots (twelfth fret). Then SLIDE!

3. Repeat (1).

4. Play open E and hold it.

Too Tall's Slide

53 1. Listen

54 2. Play

TOO TALL'S SLIDE

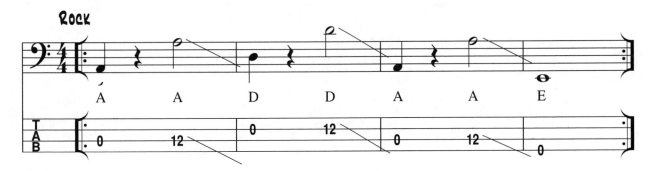

Growing the Riff

This next tune uses octaves on three strings.

Too Tall's Tale

55 **1. Listen**

56 **2. Play**

TOO TALL'S TALE

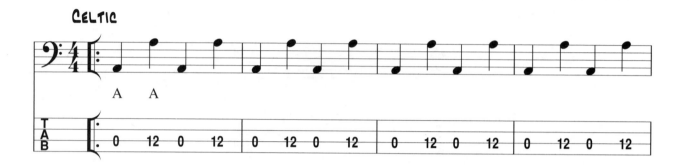

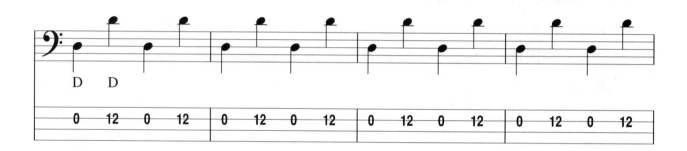

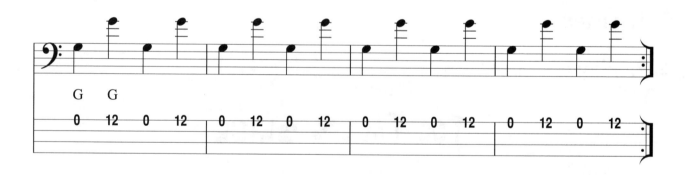

Fretboard Pattern: Octaves

You can play an octave of any note, not just open-string notes. Finger the higher octave up two strings, over two frets.

This next tune uses octaves on the first and second dots.

1. Play C on the A string, first dot (third fret). Then play its octave C on the G string, second dot (fifth fret).

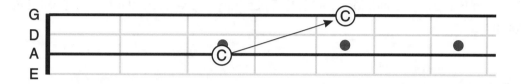

2. Play G on the E string, first dot (third fret). Then play its octave G on the D string, second dot (fifth fret).

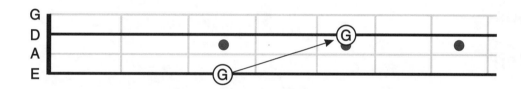

Dot's Octaves

57 **1. Listen**

58 **2. Play**

DOT'S OCTAVES

PSYCHEDELIC ROCK

Growing the Riff

This tune has the same pattern as "Dot's Octaves," but it starts on the fifth fret. Remember the octave fretboard pattern.

1. Play D on the A string, second dot (fifth fret). Then play octave D on the G string, third dot (seventh fret).

2. Play A on the E string, second dot (fifth fret). Then play octave A on the D string, third dot (seventh fret).

Octopus

59 1. Listen

60 2. Play

OCTOPUS

PSYCHEDELIC ROCK

D   D   A   A

7   7
5   5

Jimi's Tune

This tune combines the octaves from the last two tunes.

61 **1. Listen**

62 **2. Play**

JIMI'S TUNE

PSYCHEDELIC ROCK

C C G G D D A A E E

> **Challenge:** Once you have "Jimi's Tune" down, try sliding around the neck to spice it up.

> ### On the Scene
>
> *Rock guitarist Jimi Hendrix inspired many musicians.*
> *His bass players were Noel Redding and Billy Cox.*

Growing the Riff

In this tune, you play octaves all around the fretboard.

1. Play G, A, and B on the E string.

2. Find their octaves: up two strings, over two frets.

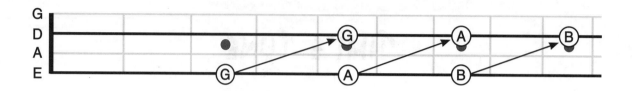

Encore Octaves

63 1. Listen

64 2. Play

ENCORE OCTAVES

REGGAE ROCK

Nice Show!

Author's Note

Thanks for playing *Instant Bass*. I hope you had fun with the songs. The bass patterns you've learned in this book (whole steps, half steps, fifths, octaves, slides) are actually used in most of your favorite songs. Lots of music has the bass playing repetitive patterns, just like the songs in this book.

Try playing along with any music and see if you can find where these patterns fit in. Sometimes you have to move the patterns to different locations on the fretboard to make the music sound good. Trial and error eventually will lead you towards knowing where and when to use these patterns, and others.

You have begun to hear how the bass functions in music. Also, your hands are becoming comfortable with the fretboard and the strings. Your bass playing will get stronger the more you do it.

Experimenting with bass lines will lead you to discover new patterns. Once you uncover a good pattern, stick to it and build a solid foundation with the drums. Good rhythm section (bass and drum) players know how to communicate through music, the language of rhythm and harmony.

I hope music and bass playing enrich your life as they have mine.

Take care,

Danny

Berklee Press DVDs:
Just Press PLAY

Kenwood Dennard:
The Studio/ Touring Drummer

| ISBN: 0-87639-022-X | HL: 50448034 | DVD $19.95 |

The Ultimate Practice
Guide for Vocalists

| ISBN: 0-87639-035-1 | HL: 50448017 | DVD $19.95 |

Featuring Donna McElroy

Real-Life Career Guide for the
Professional Musician

| ISBN: 0-87639-031-9 | HL: 50448013 | DVD $19.95 |

Featuring David Rosenthal

Essential Rock Grooves for Bass

| ISBN: 0-87639-037-8 | HL: 50448019 | DVD $19.95 |

Featuring Danny Morris

Jazz Guitar Techniques: Modal Voicings

| ISBN: 0-87639-034-3 | HL: 50448016 | DVD $19.95 |

Featuring Rick Peckham

Jim Kelly's Guitar Workshop

| ISBN: 0-634-00865-X | HL: 00320168 | DVD $19.95 |

Latin Jazz Grooves
Featuring Victor Mendoza

| ISBN: 0-87639-002-5 | HL: 50448003 | DVD $19.95 |

Basic Afro-Cuban Rhythms for
Drum Set and Hand Percussion

| ISBN: 0-87639-030-0 | HL: 50448012 | DVD $19.95 |

Featuring Ricardo Monzón

Vocal Technique: Developing
Your Voice for Performance

| ISBN: 0-87639-026-2 | HL: 50448038 | DVD $19.95 |

Featuring Anne Peckham

Preparing for Your Concert

| ISBN: 0-87639-036-X | HL: 50448018 | DVD $19.95 |

Featuring JoAnne Brackeen

Jazz Improvisation: Starting Out with
Motivic Development

| ISBN: 0-87639-032-7 | HL: 50448014 | DVD $19.95 |

Featuring Ed Tomassi

Chop Builder for Rock Guitar

| ISBN: 0-87639-033-5 | HL: 50448015 | DVD $19.95 |

Featuring "Shred Lord" Joe Stump

Turntable Technique: The Art of the DJ

| ISBN: 0-87639-038-6 | HL: 50448025 | DVD $24.95 |

Featuring Stephen Webber

Jazz Improvisation: A Personal
Approach with Joe Lovano

| ISBN: 0-87639-021-1 | HL: 50448033 | DVD $19.95 |

Harmonic Ear Training

| ISBN: 0-87639-027-0 | HL: 50448039 | DVD $19.95 |

Featuring Roberta Radley

HAL•LEONARD®